Mary Had a Little Lamb and Other Poems

Sarah Josepha Hale

DODO PRESS

MARY HAD A LITTLE LAMB
Originally called Mary's Lamb (from Poems for our children (1830))

Mary had a little lamb,
  Its fleece was white as snow,
And every where that Mary went
  The lamb was sure to go;
He followed her to school one day—-
  That was against the rule,
It made the children laugh and play,
  To see a lamb at school.

And so the Teacher turned him out,
  But still he lingered near,
And waited patiently about,
  Till Mary did appear;
And then he ran to her, and laid
  His head upon her arm,
As if he said—-'I'm not afraid—-
  You'll keep me from all harm.'
'What makes the lamb love Mary so?'
  The eager children cry—-

'O, Mary loves the lamb, you know,'
  The Teacher did reply;—-
'And you each gentle animal
  In confidence may bind,
And make them follow at your call,
  If you are always kind .'

1

IRON

"Truth shall spring out of the earth."-Psalms, lxxxv.11.

As, in lonely thought, I pondered
On the marv'lous things of earth,
And, in fancy's dreaming, wondered
At their beauty, power, and worth,
Came, like words of prayer, the feeling-
Oh! that God would make me know,
Through the spirit's clear revealing-
What, of all his works below,
Is to man a boon the greatest,
Brightening on from age to age,
Serving truest, earliest, latest,
Through the world's long pilgrimage.
Soon vast mountains rose before me,
Shaggy, desolate and lone,
Their scarred heads were threat'ning o'er me,
Their dark shadows round me thrown;
Then a voice, from out the mountains,
As an earthquake shook the ground,
And like frightened fawns the fountains,
Leaping, fled before the sound;
And the Anak oaks bowed lowly,
Quivering, aspen-like, with fear-
While the deep response came slowly,
Or it must have crushed mine ear!
"Iron! Iron! Iron!"-crashing,
Like the battle-axe and shield;
Or the sword on helmet clashing,
Through a bloody battle-field:

"Iron! Iron! Iron!"-rolling,
Like the far-off cannon's boom;
Or the death-knell, slowly tolling,
Through a dungeon's charnel gloom!
"Iron! Iron! Iron!"-swinging,
Like the summer winds at play;
Or as bells of Time were ringing
In the blest Millennial Day!
Then the clouds of ancient fable
Cleared away before mine eyes;
Truth could tread a footing stable
O'er the gulf of mysteries!
Words, the prophet bards had uttered,
Signs, the oracle foretold,
Spells, the weird-like Sibyl muttered,
Through the twilight days of old,
Rightly read, beneath the splendor,
Shining now on history's page,
All their faithful witness render-
All portend a better age.
Sisyphus, for ever toiling,
Was the type of toiling men,
While the stone of power, recoiling,
Crushed them back to earth again!
Stern Prometheus, bound and bleeding,
Imaged man in mental chain,
While the vultures, on him feeding,
Were the passions' vengeful reign;
Still a ray of mercy tarried
On the cloud, a white-winged dove,
For this mystic faith had married
Vulcan to the Queen of Love!
Rugged strength and radiant beauty-
These were one in nature's plan;

Humble toil and heavenward duty-
These will form the perfect man!
Darkly was this doctrine taught us
By the gods of heathendom;
But the living light was brought us,
When the gospel morn had come!
How the glorious change, expected,
Could be wrought, was then made free;
Of the earthly, when perfected,
Rugged Iron forms the key!
"Truth from out the earth shall flourish,"
This the Word of God makes known,-
Thence are harvests men to nourish-
There let Iron's power be shown.
Of the swords, from slaughter gory,
Ploughshares forge to break the soil;-
Then will Mind attain its glory,
Then will Labor reap the spoil,-
Error cease the soul to wilder,
Crime be checked by simple good,
As the little coral builder
Forces back the furious flood.
While our faith in good grows stronger,
Means of greater good increase;
Iron, slave of war no longer,
Leads the onward march of peace;
Still new modes of service finding,
Ocean, earth, and air it moves,
And the distant nations binding,
Like the kindred tie it proves;
With its Atlas-shoulder sharing
Loads of human toil and care;
On its wing of lightning bearing
Thought's swift mission through the air!

As the rivers, farthest flowing,
In the highest hills have birth;
As the banyan, broadest growing,
Oftenest bows its head to earth,-
So the noblest minds press onward,
Channels far of good to trace;
So the largest hearts bend downward,
Circling all the human race;
Thus, by Iron's aid, pursuing
Through the earth their plans of love,
Men our Father's will are doing,
Here, as angels do above!

BONDS

"He is a freeman whom the truth makes free,
And all are slaves beside."
Cowper

Ye may place the trusty guard,
Bolt the dark and narrow room,
Bind the heavy fetter hard,
Till the links the flesh consume;
Never, never, thus confined,
Will enslaved the prisoner be-
There's no fetter on his mind;
And the spirit will be free,-
If stern memory's thrilling tone
Wake no terrors in his heart;
In the visioned future, shown,
If he act the lofty part.
Ye may bar him from the air,
And the light of heaven forbid,-
There's a region fresh and fair,
And its smile can ne'er be hid
From the meek and trusting eyes,
Looking upward steadily;
And his thoughts will thus arise,
Till he triumphs with the free,-
If his soul have never bowed
When a golden Image shone-
If among the servile crowd,
He would follow Truth alone.
Ye may deck the lofty hall
With the wealth of earth and sea,

And, in splendor over all
Wave the banners of the free-
Ye may crown the conqueror there,
With the laurels of the brave;
'Mid the honors ye prepare,
He shall feel himself a slave,-
If ambition rule his thought,
And the highest place he ask,
All the labors he has wrought
Are but scourges to his task.
Ye may twine the living flowers
Where the living fountains glide,
And beneath the rosy bowers
Let the selfish man abide,
And the birds upon the wing,
And the barks upon the wave,
Shall no sense of freedom bring;
All is slavery to the slave!
Mammon's close-linked bonds have bound him,
Self-imposed, and seldom burst;
Though heaven's waters gush around him,
He would pine with earth's poor thirst.

THE SILK-WORM

There is no form upon our earth
That bears the mighty Maker's seal,
But has some charm:-to draw this forth,
We must have hearts to feel.
I saw a fair young girl-her face
Was sweet as dream of cherished friend-
Just at the age when childhood's grace
And maiden softness blend.
A silk-worm in her hand she laid,
Nor fear, nor yet disgust was stirred;
But gaily with her charge she played,
As 'twere a nestling bird.
She raised it to her dimpled cheek,
And let it rest and revel there,-
O, why for outward beauty seek-
Love makes its favourites fair!
That worm-I should have shrunk, in truth,
To feel the reptile o'er me move;
But, loved by innocence and youth,
I deemed it worthy love.
Would we, I thought, the soul imbue,
In early life, with sympathies
For every harmless thing, and view
Such creatures formed to please:
And when with usefulness combined,
Give them our love and gentle care-
O, we might have a world as kind
As God has made it fair!
There is no form upon our earth,
Bearing the mighty Maker's seal,

But has some charm:-to call this forth
We need but hearts to feel.

THE TWO MAIDENS

One came with light and laughing air,
And cheek like opening blossom,-
Bright gems were twined amid her hair,
And glittered on her bosom,
And pearls and costly diamonds deck
Her round, white arms and lovely neck.
Like summer's sky, with stars bedight,
The jewelled robe around her,
And dazzling as the noontide light
The radiant zone that bound her,-
And pride and joy were in her eye,
And mortals bowed as she passed by.
Another came-o'er her sweet face
A pensive shade was stealing;
Yet there no grief of earth we trace-
But the heaven-hallowed feeling
Which mourns the heart should ever stray
From the pure fount of Truth away.
Around her brow, as snow-drop fair,
The glossy tresses cluster,
Nor pearl, nor ornament was there,
Save the meek spirit's lustre;-
And faith and hope beamed in her eye,
And angels bowed as she passed by.

THE EMPIRE OF WOMAN

1.
Woman's Empire defined.
The outward World, for rugged Toil designed,
Where Evil from true Good the crown hath riven,
Has been to Man's dominion ever given;
But Woman's empire, holier, more refined,
Moulds, moves and sways the fall'n but God-breathed mind,
Lifting the earth-crushed heart to hope and heaven:
As plants put forth to Summer's gentle wind,
And 'neath the sweet, soft light of starry even,
Those treasures which the tyrant Winter's sway
Could never wrest from Nature,-so the soul
Will Woman's sweet and gentle power obey-
Thus doth her summer smile its strength control;
Her love sow flowers along life's thorny way;
Her star-bright faith lead up toward heaven's goal.

2.
The Daughter.
The iron cares that load and press men down
A father can, like school-boy tasks, lay by,
When gazing in his Daughter's loving eye,
Her soft arm like a spell around him thrown:
The passions that, like Upas' leaves, have grown
Most deadly in dark places, which defy
Earth, heaven and human will, even these were shown
All powerless to resist the pleading cry
Which pierced a savage but a father's ear,
And shook a soul where pity's pulse seemed dead;
When Pocahontas, heeding not the fear

That daunted boldest warriors, laid her head
Beside the doomed! Now with our country's fame,
Sweet forest* Daughter, we have blent thy name.

* See the splendid painting, "Baptism of Pocahontas," at the
Capitol. [Hale's note.]

3.
The Sister.
Wild as a cold, o'er prairies bounding free,
The wakened spirit of the Boy doth spring,
Spurning the rein authority would fling,
And striving with his peers for mastery;
But in the household gathering let him see
His Sister's winning smile, and it will bring
A change o'er all his nature; patiently,
As cagéd bird, that never used its wing,
He turns him to the tasks that she doth share-
His better feelings kindle by her side-
Visions of angel beauty fill the air,-
And she may summon such to be his guide:-
Our Saviour listened to a Sister's prayer,
When, "Lazarus, from the tomb come forth!" he cried.

4.
The Wife.
The Daughter from her father's bosom goes-
The Sister drops her brother's clasping hand-
For God himself ordained a holier band
Than kindred blood on human minds bestows:
That stronger, deeper, dearer tie she knows,
The heart-wed Wife; as heaven by rainbow spanned,
Thus bright with hope life's path before her glows-
Proves it like mirage on the desert's sand?

Still in her soul the light divine remains-
And if her husband's strength be overborne
By sorrow, sickness, or the felon's chains,-
Such as by England's noblest son* were worn,-
Unheeding how her own poor heart is torn,
She, angel-like, his sinking soul sustains.

Lord William Russell. [Hale's note.] Lord William Russell (1639-1683), imprisoned in the Tower of London and executed on charges of treason against King Charles II, was posthumously revered as a Protestant martyr. His wife, Lady Rachel Wriothesley Russell (1636-1723), aided in his defense in the courtroom and through letters, which were collected and published (1773, 1819, 1853).

5.
The Mother.
Earth held no symbol, had no living sign
To image forth the Mother's deathless love;
And so the tender care the righteous prove
Beneath the ever-watching eye divine,
Was given a type to show how pure a shrine,
The Mother's heart, was hallowed from above;
And how her mortal hopes must intertwine
With hopes immortal,-and she may not move
From this high station which her Saviour sealed,
When in maternal arms he lay revealed.
Oh! wondrous power, how little understood,
Entrusted to the Mother's mind alone,
To fashion genius, form the soul for good,
Inspire a West,* or train a Washington!

* *My mother's kiss made me a painter, was the testimony of this great artist. [Hale's note.]*

EIGHTEEN HUNDRED AND THIRTY

We bring no earthly wreath for Time;
To man th'immortal Time was given-
Years should be marked by deeds sublime,
That elevate his soul to heaven.
Thou proudly passing year-thy name
Is registered in mind's bright flame,
And louder than the roar of waves,
Thundering from ocean's prison caves,
Comes the glad shout that hallows thee
The Year of Freedom's Jubilee!
'Tis strange how mind has been chained down,
And reason scourged like branded sin!
How man has shrunk before man's frown,
And darkened heaven's own fire within!
But Freedom breathed-the flame burst forth-
Wo to the spoilers of the earth,
Who would withstand its lightning stroke,
And heavier forge the galling yoke;-
As well the breaking reed might dare
The cataract's rush-the whirlwind's war!
Ay, thrones must crumble-even as clay,
Searched by the scorching sun and wind!
And crushed be Superstition's sway
That would with writing scorpions bind
The terror-stricken conscience down
Beneath anointed monarch's frown;
Till Truth is in her temple sought,
The soul's unbribed, unfettered thought,
That, science-guided, soars unawed,
And reading Nature rests on God!

This must be-is-the passing year
Has rent the veil, and despots stand
In the keen glance of Truth severe,
With craven brow and palsied hand:-
Ye, who would make man's spirit free,
And change the Old World's destiny,
Bring forth from Learning's halls the light,
And watch, that Virtue's shield be bright;
Then to the "God of order" raise
The vow of faith, the song of praise,
And on-and sweep Oppression's chains,
Like ice beneath the vernal rains!
My Country, ay, thy sons are proud,
True heirs of Freedom's glorious dower;
For never here has knee been bowed
In homage to a mortal power:
No, never here has tyrant reigned,
And never here has thought been chained!
Then who would follow Europe's sickly light,
When here the soul may put forth all her might,
And show the nations, as they gaze in awe,
That Wisdom dwells with Liberty and Law!
O, when will Time his holiest triumph bring-
"Freedom o'er all the earth, and Christ alone reigns King!"

STANZAS TO THE MEMORY OF L.E.L.

[Written immediately after reading the confirmation of the rumor that Miss Maclean, better known as Miss Landon, had died at Cape Town, Africa.]

And thou art gone! the Bridal Rose
Fresh on thy laurelled head;
A land of new, wild, wondrous scenes
Before thy fancy spread-
Song on thy lip.-It may not be;-
I scarce believe thee dead!
"Bring flowers, pale flowers!"-But who for thee
An offering meet can bring?
Who paint thy Muse, like Huma* bright,
For ever on the wing?
Or catch the tones that thrilled the soul,
Poured from thy Lyre's sweet string?
They say thy heart's warm buds of hope
Had never felt a blight;
That 'mid gay throngs, in brilliant halls,
Thy step was ever light,
At gatherings round the social hearth
None wore a smile more bright.
And yet, upon thy world of song,
Dark shadows always sleep;
The beings by thy fancy formed,
Seemed only born to weep,-
Why did thy Soul's sweet fountains pour
A tide of grief so deep?
Was the prophetic shadow cast
By Afric's land of gloom;
That thus thy fancy ever linked

The poison with the bloom?
And 'mid the fairest bowers of bliss
Still reared the lonely tomb?
In vain we search for Thought's deep source,
Its mysteries none can tell;
We only know thy dreams were sad,
And so it has befell
That Love's bright wreath crowned thee for Death!
-Dark fate-and yet 'tis well:-
Ay, well for thee; thy strength had failed
To bear the Exile's chain,
The weary, pining, homesick lot,
That withers heart and brain,-
And He, who framed thy soul's fine pulse,
In mercy spared the pain.
And while we mourn a Pleiad lost
From out Mind's lofty sky,
A Lyre unstrung, whose "charméd chords"
Breathed strains that ne'er can die,
Give us, O God, the faith that sees
The Spirit's Home on high.
Sweet Minstrel of the heart, farewell;
How many grieve for thee!
What kings might ne'er command is thine,
Love's tribute from the Free:
The flowery earth, the starry sky,
The mourner's tear, the lover's sigh,
Enshrine thy memory.
And this is fame! The glorious meed
Is thine beyond decay,
Landon will grace the Briton's lore
Till earth shall pass away;
What India's wealth were poor to buy
Won by a Woman's lay!

* *Huma-a bird of the East, which the natives say never rests, as it is only seen flying. [Hale's note]*

ALICE RAY: A ROMANCE IN RHYME

"Break, Phantasy, from thy cave of cloud,
And spread thy purple wings!-
Now all thy figures are allowed,
And various shapes of things."
Ben Jonson

CANTO I.
ALICE AT HOME.
The birds their love-notes warble
Among the blossomed trees;
The flowers are sighing forth their sweets
To wooing honey-bees;-
The glad brook o'er a pebbly floor
Goes dancing on its way,-
But not a thing is so like spring
As happy Alice Ray.
An only child was Alice,
And, like the blest above,
The gentle maid had ever breathed
An atmosphere of love;
Her father's smile like sunshine came,
Like dew her mother's kiss,
Their love and goodness made her home,
Like heaven, the place of bliss.
Beneath such tender training,
The joyous child had sprung
Like one bright flower, in wild-wood bower,
And gladness round her flung;
And all who met her blessed her,

And turned again to pray,
That grief and care might ever spare
The happy Alice Ray.
The gift that made her charming
Was not from Venus caught;
Nor was it, Pallas-like, derived
From majesty of thought;-
Her healthful cheek was tinged with brown,
Her hair without a curl;
But then her eyes were love-lit stars,
Her teeth as pure as pearl.
And when in merry laughter
Her sweet, clear voice was heard,
It welled from out her happy heart
Like carol of a bird;
And all who heard were moved to smiles,
As at some mirthful lay,
And, to the stranger's look, replied-
"'Tis that dear Alice Ray."
And so she came, like sunbeams
That bring the April green;
As type of nature's royalty,
They called her "Woodburn's Queen!"
A sweet, heart-lifting cheerfulness,
Like spring-time of the year,
Seemed ever on her steps to wait,-
No wonder she was dear.
Yet though with nature living,
And little taught by rules,
Her mind had often grasped a truth
Beyond the art of schools;-
No Sophist could have moved her faith,-
She knew her Bible true,
And thrice, ere sixteen springs she bloomed,

Had read the good Book through.
In sooth, books oft beguiled her
From work as well as play,
And in their dear companionship
She passed the live-long day-
Sweet Poesy and wild Romance,
Tales of the Wise and Good,
Poor Christian's weary Pilgrimage,
And "Sweetened Solitude."
And, with the Story-tellers,
What friendships had she made!
She pitied lonely Crusoe's lot,
And loved Scheherazade,-
But to the Bard of Avon turned
Her fancy and her heart,
Nor knew which most in him she loved-
The nature or the art.
Her world was ever joyous-
She thought of grief and pain
As giants in the olden time
That ne'er would come again;
The seasons all had charms for her;
She welcomed each with joy,-
The charm that in her spirit lived
No changes could destroy.
Her heart was like a fountain,
The waters always sweet,-
Her pony in the pasture,
The kitten at her feet,
The ruffling bird of June, and
The wren in the old wall-
Each knew her loving carefulness,
And came at her soft call.
Her love made all things lovely,

For in the heart must live
The feeling that imparts the charm-
We gain by what we give.
She never thought of ugliness
Unless with sin conjoined,-
How could dark Envy's shadow creep
On such a warm, pure mind?
And who could dream the future
Had ills for her in store?
Her cup of life seemed filled from springs
With pure joy brimming o'er-
And Piety, like living plant,
Beside the waters rose,
With healing leaves to shelter her
From every storm that blows.
And though, as years rolled onward,
Her parents might be gone,
Yet still the loving Alice
Would never be alone.
Was not young Arthur even now
For ever by her side?
They were too young to marry yet,
But she would be his bride:
So thought the town of Woodburn,
And all the gossips cried-
"A noble Bridegroom he will make!
And she a charming Bride!"
The son of good old Deacon Gray-
And vainly had you gone,
To find a youth like Arthur,
From Maine to Galveston.
He won the prize at college
And in the wrestler's ring;
Could shoot a squirrel in the eye,

Or woodcock on the wing;
He rode with grace and bearing high,
Like Cossack in command;
And his good steed would gently feed,
Like Arab's, from his hand;
And, when he called his dog or steed,
His tones were ever bland.
And he the Law was reading,
And all the neighbours said,-
"He'll make a Judge like Marshall,
With such a heart and head!"
Aunt Mary said the orphan
Would find a friend in him,
For when she told a moving tale,
His eyes with tears were dim.
The brave are ever gentle,
The good should be the gay,-
And Arthur was as bold of heart
As knight in tourney fray,-
His mind was always firm for truth
As rock 'mid ocean's spray;
And, though a restless daring will
At times he might display,
His wildest moods were calmed at once,
But mention Alice Ray.
And she-though when you talked of him,
She blushed and turned away-
Was still his partner in the dance
And in the dashing sleigh;
-They always searched together
For flowers the first of May;
And duly to the Sabbath School
On every holy day

She went-they both were Teachers there,-
She went with Arthur Gray.

CANTO II.
THE TEMPTATION.
Pale Zephyrus is yielding
His last and sweetest sighs,
And Autumn's mist-like veil is drawn
Athwart the summer skies,
A veil as for a Bride's fair face,
Which loveliness conceals,
And wakens Fancy more than all
That Summer's pride reveals.
What though the thick-leaved forest
Has lost its lustrous green;
And on the meadow's sobered breast
A shade of brown is seen;-
We greet, with double blessings,
The bright-eyed gipsy flowers,
That, from departing Summer's hand,
Seem sown in rainbow showers.
We watch the lights and shadows
That frolic o'er the hills,
And deeper sense of Beauty's power
The yearning spirit fills;-
If God through every change can keep
This earth so good and fair,
We raise our eyes towards heaven and say-
"What Beauty must be there!"
While thus the face of nature
Was beautiful to see,
Young Alice wept in sorrow
Beneath the old elm-tree;
A wild bird was above her head,

And by her side a flower,-
Oh how has nature o'er her heart
Thus lost its charm and power?
She has been to Saratoga,
Where crowds of Fashion press,
And her dear, cherished home no more
Has light and pleasantness;
But deadlier still the poison
That such deep suffering stirs-
The power of Beauty she has seen,
And felt it was not hers!
She has seen the fair Belinda,
-So exquisitely fair!-
Like alabaster flushed with life;
And then her glorious hair,
It clustered round her lovely neck
Like tendrils round a vine,-
And Alice sighed in bitterness-
"Oh, were such beauty mine!"
Yet not the pride of conquest
Her troubled bosom filled-
The fear she should not be beloved,
-'Twas this her being chilled;
"Even Arthur Gray," thus ran her thoughts,
"Some fairer girl may spy,-
Or leave me for Belinda;-
Oh, if I could but die!"
While thus her heart was wrestling
With its first crushing fear,
A Voice of stern command out-spoke,
Close to her startled ear,-
"Go, Maiden, to the Haunted Dell,
And in the 'Bloody Spring,'
Where the spotted toad sits drinking,

And the night-bat laves its wing,
And adder snakes are coiling,
Bathe thou thy face and hair-
Bathe thrice, not breathe a word or sound,
And then thou shalt be fair!"
She started from the Tempter!-
Her heart grew stony cold;
She knew such gossip stories-
There was a legend old,
How a maid of peerless beauty
Was murdered in that Dell
By wily, ruthless savages,-
And how her fair face fell
In a lone Spring, thence "Bloody" called,-
And those who found her there,
And drew her gently forth, their hands
Had all waxed wondrous fair.
Yet still she felt 'twas sinful
To try such awful spell,
'Twas plain that naught but evil
Could live in that lone dell;
No human foot approached it-
'Twas far, and wild the way;
How could she venture there alone,
This timid Alice Ray?
But still the wish was rising-
Oh, that she could be fair!
She looked towards the haunted dell,-
'Twas not such distance there;
The sun was still above the hill,
And she, before 'twas night,
Might go and come, and know her doom-
But then, would this be right?
She thought of all strange stories

That she had read or heard.
Of Cinderella's Fairy kind,
And of the "talking bird"-
Of "Undine" from her ocean home,
Wild Fancy's loveliest child,-
And then she thought of "water cures,"-
No dream could be more wild!
But yet she knew her Bible
Would never bid her go;
It could not be an angel
Was keeping watch below,
And, pitying her hopeless grief,
Was counselling its cure-
Oh, no, 'twas not an angel-
'Twas some foul demon sure!
Such demon as in olden times
Had lured young girls away,
In guise of gallant Troubadour,
Or holy Friar grey,
And now was lurking round her path,
Her precious soul to win;
And should she listen to his wiles,
And do this deadly sin?
She hurried to her chamber,
To 'scape the dreadful snare,-
The words of that commanding Voice
Seemed sounding even there,-
"Go, maiden, to the 'Bloody Spring,'
And bathe thy face and hair,
Bathe thrice, nor breathe a sound nor word,
-Thou shalt be wondrous fair."

CANTO III.
THE HAUNTED DELL
When soft the gales are blowing,
And calm is ocean's wave,
So small the danger seemeth
That every heart is brave;-
But let the tempest rise in wrath,
The ocean flout the sky,-
The firmest shriek, in agony,
"Lord, save us, or we die!"
And while in peace abiding,
Within a sheltered home,
We feel as sin and evil
Could never, never come;-
But let the strong temptation rise,
As whirlwinds sweep the sea-
We find no strength to 'scape the wreck,
Save, pitying God, in Thee.
Wise men have worshipped Mammon,
And lost their souls for gold;
Pure women, for the pride of life,
Their priceless hearts have sold;
And for revenge, or power, or fame,
What deeds are done each day,-
And all by beings, guiltless once
As gentle Alice Ray!
Then blame not too severely
The wish of this young girl
To have a face as fair as day,
And hair of graceful curl!
She fondly trusts by Beauty's power
Her Lover's heart to bind,-
For this, for this she trembling goes
The "Bloody Spring" to find.

And she has crossed the brooklet,
And scaled the mountain steep,
And down, and downward winds her path,
Into a valley deep-
Above her crowd the fir trees,
Dark, motionless, and tall,
She hears no sound on that lone ground,
Save her own light foot-fall.
And thrice her step hath stumbled
O'er deadly hemlock roots;
And thrice the poison ivy
Hath clasped her with its shoots;
And thrice a white owl hooted,
Close to her throbbing ear,
And seemed to ask her conscience,
What dost thou, Maiden, here?
Still on-the Dell is entered,
And reached the "Bloody Spring,"
And here she nearly fainted-
She felt the night-bat's wing
Cold on her cheek-yet down she stooped
And bathed her face and hair;
And all around was lone and still
As Death were watching there!
Again, but very slowly,
She bends as with a load-
Well may she start and shudder-
She grasped the slimy toad;
-But cast it from her, like a stone,
And bathed her face and hair;
And all around was dark and still
As Death were listening there.
Again, but slow and slower,
She bendeth o'er the Spring,-

The bat is wheeling round and round,
She feels its clammy wing;-
The toad is creeping o'er her foot-
Yet mindful of the charm,
She bore her bravely till she felt
The snakes coil round her arm!
Oh! then she lost her footing,
And prone she would have sunk,
But for a black-thorn's ragged branch-
Sole branch from rotting trunk;
She grasped it in her agony,
The foul snakes dropped away,-
And with her arms all bleeding,
Fled fainting Alice Ray.
She reached her home scarce living,-
But when the morning shone,
And she her faithful mirror sought-
How fair her face had grown!
The freckles all had vanished,
Her cheek was like the dawn,
The blush half struggling through the light,
Like rose-leaf under lawn.
And then her hair was flowing,
And kept in curl so long;
How could she think the spell had been
So very, very wrong!
The treacherous heart will deem success
Has sanctified the deed;
The first step costs-but easy then
Sin's downward path will lead,-
This moral from her story learn,
-Of thy first step take heed.
For oh, what worldly passions
Were working in her breast!

What dreams of ball-room conquests
Now broke her pillowed rest!
Her pony whinnied as she passed-
She never seemed to hear;
Her birds came round-she strewed no seeds,
And they withdrew in fear;
Her books had lost their charm and power,
And even her Bible lay
Unopened near her toilet glass-
Wo! wo! for Alice Ray.
Then flatterers flocked around her,
In proud and rich array;
And every day her charms increased,
Like some rare flower of May,
That opened later than the rest,
The sooner will decay;-
Still she was true to Arthur,
And might have been alway;
But from the city's courtly ranks
A lover rich and gay,
Smit with her face and flowing curls,
His homage came to pay.
And princely in his port was he,
And winning in his way,
And versed in love's seductive wiles,
He knew just what to say,-
And so he won fair Alice-
How could she say him, "nay"!-
And she has left her dear, dear home,
Home of her infant play
And childhood's joy;-but there are ties
Which never can decay;
However dear new friends may be,
However far she stray,

She yet will see her Mother weep,
And hear her Father pray,-
Praying for her happiness,
Weeping in dismay,
That she, their dear and only child,
Must go so far away!-
She bade farewell to them, to all-
Farewell to Arthur Gray.

CANTO IV.
THE RETRIBUTION.
Around the sides of Etna
How fair the gardens grow,-
Yet burning Desolation
Is fierce and near below!-
While straying 'mid the vines and flowers,
We rarely pause to think,
How close this Beauty presses on
Destruction's awful brink!
And when the gay are flaunting,
Like flowers from hot-house brought,
We oft forget their blandest smile
Conceals some burning thought
Of pain, remorse or envy,
The surface hid beneath,-
Oh many wear the flowers without
Whose hearts are filled with death!
When all looks fair in seeming,
And outwardly serene,
We say "'tis good;"-but had we power
To lift the veil between,
And see how passion's lava
Is gathering in the breast,
While Justice, like a hidden stream

That cannot be suppressed,
Is wearing channels, day by day,
And coming nigh and nigher,-
How we should warn the world to flee
From sin's volcanic fire!
Ay, Justice, who evades her?
Her scales reach every heart;
The action and the motive,
She weigheth each apart;
And none who swerve from right or truth
Can 'scape her penalty;-
Oh! sore the Retribution,
Poor Alice, laid on thee.
Yet Alice had not broken
A law that men endite;
But still, in her own mind she saw
The Law in purer light;
Had she not pined for Beauty,
With Envy's selfish eye,
And wed a man she did not love
For wealth, and station high?
She knew she did not love him,
Not with that pure, heart-love,
A true wife for her husband feels,
Kindled from heaven above:-
To wed a man one does not love,
What suffering to incur!
But Alice had another grief-
Her husband loved not her:-
That is,-'twas not his nature
To love with constancy;
When dazzled by her beauty,
And she a novelty,
He loved,-but soon the holy charm

Had lost its light and power,
And he would leave her lone and sad
For some new toy or flower.
She felt the change as woman
Feels, with the deepest pain,
And often strove, by sweetest wiles,
To lure his heart again;-
She wore the colours he admired,
The jewels he had given,
And met him with a face of smiles
Even when her heart was riven.
When once she tried to tell him
How she her bird had freed,
And how it nestled in her neck-
He only cried-"Indeed!
Where is the paper? 'Tis the day
To learn whose racer wins;-
And then, tonight, with that new star,
The Opera begins."
Their souls were never mated,-
Hers centred in a home
Where all was truth and tenderness,
And none but dear ones come;
His joy was found on Pleasure's tide,
With gay companions nigh,
And should they sink, it mattered not,
If he but held a buoy;-
The motto graven on his seal
Was, "I-and only I."
What wonder that in sadness
The loving Alice pined;-
Had Heaven her lot appointed
She might have been resigned;
But 'twas the bitter chalice

Which she herself had filled,-
It was the deadly Upas plant-
Her Envy had distilled.
What cared she now for Beauty?
Her Husband marked it not,-
Her flowing hair might sweetly curl,
-Its colour he forgot;
Her face was like Belinda's fair,
And yet he turned away
And gazed, and praised some painted thing
That flaunted in the play.
Yet still the hoping Alice
Was so unused to grief,
She tried to think some good would come,
Some change would bring relief;
But days, weeks-months, are passing by,
And still her chains grow stronger;
She felt her sorrow was so great
She could not bear it longer.
And now kind thoughts of Arthur
Would with her dreamings come,
She strove to drive him from her mind-
But he was near her home,
And all she loved and sighed to see,-
As well forget her prayer
As him who often by her side
Had knelt that right to share.
And he had loved her truly,
And she to him was fair,
But now, with all her Beauty,
No one for her would care;
She felt the crisis coming,
Even her bright hopes had fled,
She wished but for her mother

To hold her throbbing head.
And when the blush of morning
Burst on the eastern sky,
The high roofs seemed like leaden weights
Upon her lifted eye,-
And when, as blessèd evening came,
She looked towards the west,
She felt as if the cold, hard walls
Were closing round her breast!
And dreadful was the struggle
Of the last dying scene,-
Oh, what despairing thoughts arose,
With tears and prayers between!
The last pang came-she gave one shriek,
As though her heart-strings broke,-
And then a hand clasped hers, and then
The breathless girl—awoke!
She woke, and there was Arthur,
Beneath that old elm tree,
With face of ashy pallor,
Beside her on his knee;-
"What ails thee, Alice, dearest?
Thy cry was strange and wild;"
She laid her head upon his breast,
And wept as weeps a child.
And ere she ceased her sobbing,
She told him all her woes,
From her Saratoga sorrows,
To that dark Vision's close:
She said-"My heart was wrong and weak,
How could I be so dull!
But now my dream has taught me this,
The loved are beautiful.
Forgive me, oh, forgive me,

My foolishness and pride!"
-He whispered he forgave her all-
And something more beside;
I could not hear distinctly,
For song began to flow,
The joyous bird was over-head,
And lovers speak so low.
But this I know-ere Autumn
Put on his Winter grey-
While yet the melted rainbow,
'Mid forest shadow lay,
And trees were flushed with glory
More rich than flowers of May-
Though very late the season
For such a grand array,
It seemed as Earth kept on her robes
For Festival display-
But on the Friday after
That bright Thanksgiving-Day,*
Had you in Woodburn village
Enquired for Alice Ray-
They would have smiled and said-"She now
Is Mrs. Arthur Gray!"

* "Thou shalt keep a fast unto me, in the end of the year, when thou hast gathered in thy labors out of the field," was the command of God to his chosen people. The "Thanksgiving-Day," established soon after the settlement of New England, by the Pilgrim Fathers, obeys this requisition of joyful gratitude, and seems the natural out-pouring of thankfulness for the abundance which in autumn is gathered into the overflowing garners of America. From New England the custom has been gradually extending itself, and last year the

38

Thanksgiving-Day was kept in twenty-one, out of the twenty-nine States. In a few more years, we hope and trust the day will become a national Jubilee. Though the appointment must be always made by the State authorities, yet this might be done in concert, and a particular day-the last Thursday in November,-might be the day in every State and Territory. Then, though the members of the same family might be too far separated to meet around one festive board, they would have the gratification of knowing that all were enjoying the blessings of the day. From the St. Johns to the Rio Grande, from the Atlantic to the Pacific border, the telegraph of human happiness would move every heart to rejoice simultaneously, and render grateful thanks to God for the blessings showered on our beloved country. [Hale's note.] (Note: Hale campaigned through several presidencies for the establishment of a national Thanksgiving Day; President Lincoln finally proclaimed the national holiday in 1863.)

THE LIGHT OF HOME

My son, thou wilt dream the world is fair,
  And thy spirit will sigh to roam,
And thou *must* go; but never, when there,
  Forget the light of Home!

Though pleasures may smile with a ray more bright,
  It dazzles to lead astray;
Like the meteor's flash, 'twill deepen the night
  When treading thy lonely way:—

But the heart of home has a constant flame,
  And purse as vestal fire—
'Twill burn, 'twill burn for ever the same,
  For nature feeds the pyre.

The sea of ambition is tempest-tossed,
  And thy hopes may vanish like foam—
When sails are shivered and compass lost,
  Then look to the light of Home!

And there, like a star through midnight cloud,
  Thou'lt see the beacon bright;
For never, till shining on thy shroud,
  Can be quenched its holy light.

The sun of fame may gild the *name*,
  But the *heart* ne'er felt its ray;
And fasion's smiles, that rich ones claim,
  Are beams of a wintry day:

How cold and dim those beams would be,

Should Life's poor wanderer come!—
My son, when the world is dark to thee,
Then turn to the light of Home.

THE WATCHER

The night was dark and fearful,
  The blast swept wailing by;
A Watcher, pale and tearful,
  Look'd forth with anxious eye;
How wistfully she gazes—
  No gleam of morn is there!
And then her heart upraises
  Its agony of prayer!

Within that dwelling lonely,
  Where want and darkness reign,
Her precious child, her only,
  Lay moaning in his pain;
And death alone can free him—
  She feels that this must be:
"But oh! for morn to see him
  Smile once again for me!"

A hundred lights are glancing
  In yonder mansion fair,
And merry feet are dancing—
  They heed not morning there.
Oh! young and lovely creatures,
  One lamp, from out your store,
Would give that poor boy's features
  To her fond gaze once more.

The morning sun is shining—
  She heedeth not its ray;
Beside her dead, reclining,
  That pale, dead mother lay!

A smile her lip was wreathing,
  A smile of hope and love,
As though she still were breathing—
  "There's light for us above!"

CPSIA information can be obtained at www.ICGtesting.com
229847LV00010B/94/P